CHRONIC HOPE:

Parenting the Addicted Child

Author:

KEVIN PETERSEN, MA, LMFT

PETERSEN FAMILY COUNSELING

www.petersenfamilycounseling.com

A Special Thank You to…

I want to thank all the people that have helped me through the process of writing this book. My wife, Amy, without you this never happens. I cannot begin to tell you how grateful I am that you asked me out.

My sister Susie, her husband Tom and my two nieces, Samantha and Macey. I am so grateful you are all in my life today. There is no greater reward of sobriety.

My father Walt, who had the courage to call me out in 1990 and offer me a solution. My mother Marge, who died of our disease in 2014, and was absolutely amazing and gave me so much.

My main man, Peter Rooney, been with me since 1982 and the best friend and cheerleader a guy could ever have.

My other main man, Duke Rumely, we hate each other one day a year and the other 364, you are my dude.

Kirk Johnson, Taylor Biskup, and Rourke Weaver for keeping me accountable and Josh Miller for being the new guy and coming up with the title of this book.

My sponsor since 1998, Jack Sindelar, you are my brother.

Jen Shivey, Alex Castro and Perla Duran for being awesome every other week and helping me stay focused.

James Roman for letting me know I can open a private practice and write a book and make it all happen.

Author's Note

I started writing this book in April 2017 with the intention to write a short book about the plan that I had created for the families that were streaming into my office and asking me the same question, "What do we do with our kid who's using and drinking is out of control?" And I wanted to share with them my experience of being from an addicted family and how they helped me get sober.

I opened my private practice in Denver, Colorado in April 2014 and from the first day forward, my clients were mainly parents that would call me and ask if they could bring their kid in to see me (the kids were 14, 18, 22, 26, 36 and up) so I could help them with their substance abuse issues. My response has always been the same, I would rather meet with the parents and the family and talk about how to address the substance abuse and the family system, not just the person using. I have always believed that you have a greater chance for success if the whole family is engaged in recovery, not just the addict.

I knew my plan had to be quick and to the point so we could triage the immediate problem and then once we put the initial fire out, we could spend more time addressing the bigger issues. My wife, Amy, convinced me that my message needed to be heard by more than one family at a time in my office. And my friend, Scott Benton, offered to show me how to write a book. I am eternally grateful to both of them for getting me started and keeping me going and not letting me quit.

I know that this book could be much longer and more detailed about the nature of addiction and family systems. It has been my experience that when a family gets into my office they are looking for immediate impact and direction, not a philosophical or an intellectual discussion. It's as if you call the fire department because your house is on fire and when they show up instead of turning on the hoses and putting out the fire, they turn around and look at you and say, "How do you think the fire got started?" or "How does your house on fire make you feel?"

I wanted to create a plan that put out the fire and then ask, "Let's talk about what we can do to make sure this does not happen again. And we need to talk about the whole family." I hope that you find this book helpful in your time of crisis. I know that this plan is not for everyone but it worked for me in 1991 and continues to work for my clients today.

Kevin Petersen, MA, LMFT

Petersen Family Counseling

Denver, CO

Table of Contents

Chapter 1

Why I got into this Business

Growing up, my household had a lot of secrets that we weren't allowed to talk about. My mom was addicted to prescription drugs; my dad was extremely codependent with her – and my sister and I didn't understand that this environment wasn't normal.

Mom had been a teacher, a piano player and had once won a Twist Dance contest in San Francisco. She grew up in McCloud, California and graduated from Chico State University, which had a reputation as a party school. From what I have been told, my mom was very outgoing and had a vibrant personality before she gave birth to my sister and me. While I'm unsure when exactly she started to use prescription drugs to manage her depression, anxiety and pain issues, I didn't grow up with the outgoing, vibrant mom many had once described her to be. Sometimes she'd start a health kick or begin meeting with a therapist and she changed into the fun woman I loved to be with. But these moments were brief and unpredictable.

Dad grew up in San Jose, California. His mom was an alcoholic and his dad was a salesman for Nabisco. As the oldest of three children, it was impressed upon my dad that he was responsible for his younger brother and sister. While he had many expectations placed upon him at an early age, I know my dad felt he never lived up to them. And similar to how he felt that his role growing up was to take care of his siblings, my dad felt that his role while I grew up meant making money to afford our Palo Alto lifestyle and taking care of my mom and all her issues.

Each day I would come home from high school to find my mom in her room with the lights off and the shades drawn, complaining of what she swore were migraines. Whether if she did have real migraines or not, my mom had several prescriptions in the medicine cabinet. At 14 years old, I couldn't pronounce the names on the bottles or determine what the drugs were used for, but it was evident these prescriptions put her in a daily stupor.

My parents met in a bar in Mountain View, California in 1962, married and moved to Palo Alto, California in 1969. Working in the profitable envelope and flat packaging industry, my father had a generous income, making it easy for my mom to never work and for my sister and me to have a comfortable, privileged lifestyle with a large home, golden retrievers and lavish vacations.

Admittedly, my family did look like we had it all: money, cars, happy kids and vacations. But it was a façade. We had a monster living in our home and no one knew about it. My mom would wear her pajamas and stay in bed all day. Very sparingly she would join us on outings to sports games or family events. And when she did join us, we were always hours late. To explain our tardiness, we always came up with an excuse. But we didn't only come up with excuses for why we were late. As the responsible, dutiful son and daughter, we were caretakers and came up with excuses for why my mom didn't join us out; excuses for why my parents couldn't answer the phone even though they were home; excuses for why I was accompanying my dad to his college alumni events and not my mom.

Continuing our caretaker roles, we often organized dinner for the family and handled common parental responsibilities, but wondered what my mom did all day to be unable to take on some of the common responsibilities of a parent. One common trait of an addict is a lack of awareness unless something directly affects the addict's own needs. And I didn't understand that my mom demonstrated this lack of awareness toward her children when she failed to demonstrate the qualities of a traditional parent – including reprimand.

One instance occurred when I received a speeding ticket and had my license suspended for 30 days. Rather than reprimand me, my mom asked that I drive her to the pharmacy to pick up her medications the day after my license was suspended. Demonstrating an addict's lack of awareness, my mom didn't care that my license was suspended – she just needed her medications. I could have gone to jail if I was stopped again but to my mom, the drugs mattered more.

It wasn't until years later did I realize I had grown up in a house of addiction. Since I was 12 years old, how I lived – with my mom's reclusive behavior and her unusual amount of prescriptions, dad's codependency and my caretaking responsibilities - was all I had ever known. We were the caretakers who cleaned up the messes and kept the secrets. My mom was the addict. Never did I question any of these signs or the caretaker-addict relationship my household held because I simply thought how my family lived was normal.

But it wasn't. And while I spent many years of my childhood as the caretaker, I soon became an addict myself.

Starting at 13 years old, I briefly drank and smoked marijuana with older guys while on camping trips with the Boy Scouts of America. But since sports and schoolwork kept me busy, I didn't lose control with alcohol or drugs until I enrolled at the University of Southern California in August 1982.

With a wealth of drugs and alcohol around me, I proceeded to drink and use drugs constantly, fail my classes and mentally distance myself from my family. Meanwhile, in Palo Alto, my parents continued their façade, but my mom didn't have me as one of her caretakers anymore. My dad threatened to leave my mom; my sister was frustrated that I wasn't there with them. She would call me, insisting I come home for summer vacation, but I dreaded it.

During my first year at USC, I kept the details about my self-destructive behavior from my family. Then in summer 1983, my father and I were on a whitewater rafting trip and met John and Cristina Noble, a couple who owned a farm outside of Granada, Spain. They invited me to live with them and work on their farm. After a quick decision that college was not for me, I purchased a plane ticket and promised my parents I'd return to USC after six months in Spain.

John and Cristina showed unmatched kindness, generosity, and hospitality, and I enjoyed working on their farm, exploring Spanish cities and forgetting college. But I returned John and Cristina's benevolence with recklessness. After several drinks one evening, I drove their car off an eight-foot embankment and totaled it. Crashing the car and reflecting on John and Cristina's kindness, I went into a shame spiral filled with uncontrolled drinking.

After six months in Spain, my parents reminded me that I had agreed to return to USC. But when I came home in December 1983, frustration set in. I enjoyed my time in Spain: I supervised projects on a farm; the work was simple; I had the freedom to do whatever I wanted. In early 1984, John and Cristina had sent a postcard to me while on a safari.

Jealous of their adventure, I turned to my mom and said, "See what I gave up to come home?"

But she merely shrugged and said, "You could have stayed as there was nothing we could have done about it."

Determined to defy my parents for the rest of my life, I vowed to never listen to them again.

Returning to USC in fall 1984, I continued to struggle with drugs and alcohol over the next four years. And soon, I couldn't register for classes due to academic probation, overdue tuition bills and unresolved misconduct issues with the Dean of Student Life.

By 1988, I had spent six years partying, using drugs, drinking incessantly and wondering when I would graduate from USC. After reviewing the paperwork to determine where I stood academically, I received a hand-written note from my academic advisor. At a high level, the note outlined that I was not enrolled at all at USC, but owed $10,000 and was still on both academic probation and behavioral probation.

As I've mentioned, one feature of an addict is a lack of awareness or denial. So it's no surprise that after reading the letter from USC, I thought to myself, *I'm graduating in May!*

The graduation festivities began, and I proceeded to rent my cap and gown, and mail invitations to family and friends, letting them know about my graduation on May 9, 1988. And no surprise, I was drunk all week leading up to the graduation ceremonies. After attending the student-wide ceremony and the smaller ceremony for the Economics Department, I proudly received my empty diploma holder and partied with my friends and family. While I expected to be cornered, called a fraud and publically humiliated at any moment, it never happened.

When I moved back to Palo Alto, I spent two years bartending and selling marijuana as I knew a steady, well-paying job wouldn't be possible unless I had truly graduated college and had a degree to prove it.

In August 1990, my family hosted a four-day family reunion in Templeton, California. I was drunk the entire time and spent most of it with my cousin Nels, wasted on the front porch of the family home. My dad offered to drive me home to Palo Alto and within the first five minutes of our four-hour drive, he turned to me.

"Kevin, you are my only son, and I love you, but I can't tolerate your drinking anymore," he said. "I know you didn't actually graduate from USC two years ago, and since then, you've sold the BMW I gave you and are bartending and wasting your life. Your mother, your sister and I are not dealing with you anymore until something changes."

This wasn't the first time my parents had tried the tough love act. They always caved eventually, so I argued with my dad during the ride home, telling him he didn't love me or trust me, and that my bad decisions were his fault. But despite my insults, he proceeded to tell me that I wasn't welcome at the house and if I did drop by unannounced, he'd call the police.

After my dad dropped me off at my apartment, I proceeded to my usual routine of drinking and using drugs, knowing that once my dad simmered down, I could talk my way out of the tough love act.

I was wrong. My dad didn't budge, and after six weeks of exile from the family, I did what all "tough guy" addicts do: I called my mom. After crying about dad's unfairness and complaining about how hard my life was, my mom didn't offer a sympathetic ear. Instead, she told me to start seeing a therapist with my dad, and then maybe he would ease up.

This was a common tactic in my family: work out your issue with a doctor or therapist, then come back to family and don't talk about it anymore. My parents had been sending me to therapists since I was 14 years old, so of course I thought I would bullshit another therapist as I had for over a decade, get my privileges back and get back to my partying.

Starting in January 1991, I met with my dad and his therapist, Dr. Julian Grodsky, every Thursday morning. And during these meetings, I began to tell the truth: I admitted to faking my graduation at USC; I owned up to the drinking and the drugs.

At the same time, my dad started to tell the truth about his life. Dad elaborated on his life growing up: how his mother was an alcoholic, his brother and his sister struggled with alcohol and his father had debilitating Parkinson's disease. And while he described the expectations placed upon him as a kid, this dynamic still existed with his mother, brother, and sister. Dad admitted that he felt like a fraud in Palo Alto, as he was a working-class kid from San Jose who didn't belong with affluent, sophisticated executives. Yet, he wanted his kids to have access to schools and a life that he didn't experience.

Then one morning in late April 1991, my parents went out of town for my mom's birthday, but I went to therapy alone. While I told Dr. Grodsky we can pick up where we left off from the previous week, Dr. Grodsky said he had something he wanted to talk about with me.

"I think you are an alcoholic and a drug addict, and you need help," he said.

This was certainly not the first time I had been told I had a problem. While everyone from friends to girlfriends, employers to health professionals had all confronted me about my drinking and drug use for years, I now couldn't disagree with Dr. Grodsky. For the previous four months, I had poured my secrets to Dr. Grodsky and my dad, so I asked what I should do. Dr. Grodsky recommended a friend of his named Dr. Barry Rosen, a specialist in alcoholism and addiction.

Admitting to my addiction felt like the weight of the world was off my shoulders. During the following week's therapy session, I admitted to my dad that I was an alcoholic, and I could see the relief in his eyes. He said something like, "That explains everything! You are just too damn smart to keep screwing up so much." And after drinking at a wedding that weekend, I began my journey to sobriety on Sunday, May 5, 1991.

I've been in all the roles within the caretaker-addict relationship: I was a caretaker for my mom; I was an addict and then the addict-turned-sober and now I am a licensed mental health professional. Maybe you've been or are in one of these roles, too.

Dr. Grodsky and my dad helped me develop a plan for sobriety, which included actually securing a degree from USC. But reenrolling into the school I had wasted six years partying in wasn't going to be easy. And I knew it would take discipline, determination, and humility, starting with a visit with the secretary of the president at USC. In hopes of securing a job at USC that would allow me to attend school part-time tuition-free, I contacted my friend, Liz King, who was the president's secretary.

After explaining my plans to seek a job and enroll at USC, Liz scheduled an appointment for me to speak to the school's president on Monday, June 3, 1991. I admitted to her that I never actually graduated, yet she simply smiled.

"There are quite a few people you will need to meet before you can enroll," Liz said. "But first, I want you to run over to the Athletic Department and meet with a friend of mine named Ron Orr."

At the Athletic Department in Heritage Hall, I thought Liz had secured a job for me at the USC Athletic Department. After being escorted to a nearby office, I met Ron: a guy who looked just like me, a former swimmer and fraternity guy – and an alcoholic.

"My name is Ron," he said, shaking my hand. "I am an alcoholic, and I would like to take you to a meeting tonight if you're available."

That Monday evening began my journey into 12-Step Programs for Addiction Recovery. While I had managed to stay sober from May 5 to June 3 on pure will-power, personal will-power wouldn't be sustainable without the power of a support system. I planned to live in my former fraternity house for the summer, as it was inexpensive and close to campus. And while the other guys living there were either working or attending summer school classes, they also partied how I used to during my first round at USC.

I soon secured a job counseling parents and students on tuition, expenses, and payments at the Office of Financial Services, working for Peter Tom. Kind, patient, and unafraid to hold me accountable, Tom supported me on my road to sobriety.

In January 1992, I began my second round as a student at USC. And I was entirely unprepared for the workload from my classes, plus my full-time job and daily 12-Step meetings. The next two and a half years had its ups and downs. Often, I felt overwhelmed with school courses and was reprimanded at work for falling behind at times. Yet the people who came into my life over those two and a half years – Dr. Grodsky, Liz, Ron, and Peter – were my personal angels who helped guide me to sobriety.

In August 1994, I graduated from USC with a Bachelor of Arts degree in Social Sciences. A year later, I moved to Colorado. My sister had moved to Boulder, Colorado in 1993, and I knew after visiting her a few times, it was where I wanted to be.

The following few years were a whirlwind. I quickly found my 12-Step community in both Denver and Boulder, lived with my cousin, Joe, and worked in a series of successful sales job roles at various companies. But when I got married in 2002 and divorced in 2005, I hit a wall in my journey of sobriety.

My ex-wife was unfaithful to me. And while I continued to step-parent my ex-wife's two children after the divorce, my ex-wife believed that given my history as an addict-turned-sober, I was still irresponsible and unreliable.

I never saw the children again – and sank into a depression that kept me in an auto-pilot motion for the next few months.

At 43 years old and 16 years sober, I was extremely unhappy. I no longer saw my step-children I loved and was burned out from the grueling sales roles that brought in a high salary with minimal personal fulfillment. Should I go back to graduate school or continue in my cushy role in sales?

I began reevaluating what did make me happy: helping others and seeing people pierce their lives together as addicts across the nation do in 12-Step Programs. For 16 years, my 12-Step meetings had kept me mentally afloat.

So what did I do? I quit my sales job and applied to a graduate program focused on counseling at Regis University. While attending an open house event, I cornered the Dean of Students, John Armand, and asked him if I was wasting their time. My academic career had ended with a 2.0 GPA at USC *after* taking all of my major courses twice, plus several electives I received a grade of an A to boost my GPA for graduation.

"Kevin, look around the room," John said. "How many men do you see here tonight?" Noticing there were about three of us out of the 35 attendees, he noticed my confusion.

"How many of these men are your age?" he went on. I was the only one. And John said, "We need more people like you, people who are seasoned and have been around the block and know what they want to do."

By graduation in August 2011, I had passed a probationary class with an A, secured a 3.85 GPA and graduated in the Honors Society as a Student Marshall.

My life has had its ups and downs, but every step brought me closer to understanding how I can help others who are struggling with loved ones who suffer from addiction. First, I was a member of an addicted family, then an addict to a sober man, to a sober man with a Master's degree in Marriage and Family Therapy.

Aside from my personal experiences, my professional experiences have furthered my understanding of mental health and addiction therapy. After graduation, Arapahoe Douglas Mental Health Network (ADMHN) hired me as a full-time case manager and outpatient therapist and a part-time mental health technician and counselor at The Bridge House, ADMHN's acute treatment unit focused on suicidal or psychotic patients after they have visited the Emergency Room.

After working part-time for three years in this capacity, I joined the Intensive Services Team and met kids in the ER who were suicidal or psychotic, evaluated them and followed them home to offer in-home family services.

After experiencing all the roles of the caretaker-addict relationship, then becoming a licensed marriage and family therapist, I understand all the scenarios – being an addict and recovering, being a caretaker and living in a house of addiction. I want to help you, your family and friends by sharing my experiences with you, whether you are the addict, the co-dependent or a mental health professional.

If you have picked up this book, you are already in the throes of dealing with an addict. And while you may have discovered your kid uses drugs, tried to set boundaries and visited countless therapists, you're at the end of your rope in determining how to change the situation.

I can help. While over the past 10 years, various methods have worked with clients, I do know that my personal experience in drugs and alcohol, plus my path to sobriety at 28 years old has helped families across the nation come to terms with their houses of addiction.

Ready to get started?

Key takeaways:

- Addiction is characterized by the inability of the addict to control the amount of substance they use and the frequency of their use.
- Addiction is actually more about the addict's life being out of control and unmanageable than substance abuse.
- Codependency is driven by the agreement that I will work harder on your problem and life than you do.
- Rescuing someone who continues to make poor choices is not called love, it's called enabling. Stop enabling and refuse to be a safety net, so they can grow up.

- I grew up in an addicted home, became an addict, got sober in 1991 and then became a mental health professional.
- Everyone I know with long-term sobriety has the same story; when their family said "enough" is when the recovery process started.

Chapter 2

Take a Step Back - Triage Your Home

The first phone call or conversation with many of my stressed, flustered and panic-stricken parents is usually a derivative of the following:

"Our kid is out of control! We've tried everything! What do we do? I want to bring my kid to see you. Maybe you can talk some sense into him."

Let's take a step back. I'd be curious to know what "everything" is you've tried. But even more than this: I don't want to see your kid. While many parents expect they can simply bring their kids to my office in hopes I would revert things back to normal, parents are so surprised when I tell them: no. No, I don't want to meet with your kid. I want to meet with *you, the parents*. And I want to meet with you alone. There will be plenty of time for family work but first, I want to meet with the management team.

At the first meeting with parents, I reiterate the fact that we're a team. And it starts with admitting that the old strategies at home haven't worked and understanding that together, we're going to find a solution that does work. Teamwork starts with an honest answer to the question: "Can we agree that the way you as parents are handling things is not working and that we need to try something new?" This question isn't meant for parents to feel defensive or at fault for their kid's addiction or behavior. Rather, parents are responsible for how they *react* to addiction and behavior.

And then I'll ask about what's been happening at home. I want the long, detailed history, not the abbreviated, short version with a few data points.

After hearing the full story, I also often learn that the parents have usually spoken to everyone in their lives: the family therapist, doctor and psychiatrist, the school counselor and school psychologist, the kid's coaches and mentors, the minister, rabbi or priest, and the elders. They have tried everything that was suggested, and still, the kid is drinking, using drugs, and wreaking havoc to their life and the family.

Experimenting vs. Abusing

To confirm, I am not describing a kid who has been experimenting a bit with drinking or smoking marijuana and then was caught at school or at a party, received a curfew violation, or received a "Minor in Possession" (MIP) ticket and needs a stern talk and some clear consequences. A kid facing that kind of problem will get their act together quickly as minor experimentation can be controlled. For example, he tried some marijuana at a party but didn't try it again, or she was sneaking beer with a friend and realized it isn't her thing. These are instances in which the kid can exhibit self-control. The important thing for parents to see: the difference between experimenting and abusing.

A kid who is experimenting typically has a good track record and gets caught at home, school or by the police at a party drinking or smoking pot. The critical thing to understand is that kids who are experimenting can take it or leave it alone, as they don't feel the need to continue experimenting after they have been caught and experienced the consequences. Their grades stay the same; they have the same peer group and friends, and their behavior at home is the same. And the key to helping a kid who is experimenting is having parents who show consistency in consequences. Too many times, I see parents who apply the consequences periodically rather than consistently, so their kid then doesn't take them seriously.

It's been my experience, both personally and professionally, that 80 to 90 percent of kids who are caught experimenting will generally abide by their parents' rules and maybe test their parents' tolerance once or twice more.

But the other 10 to 20 percent of kids fall into a potential addiction category. These are kids who continually test the boundaries, hoping their parents will grow tired of trying to hold them accountable with consequences. Some signs to look for if you suspect your kid may be in this category are new friends that are very unlike their old friends, changes in academic performance, quitting sports or other activities, and isolating in their rooms when they come home. These are all reasons for the parents to explain their concern to their kid and say, "I love you and if you don't follow the rules, we are going to start drug testing you."

Unacceptable experimentation or abuse begins the moment a kid uses drugs or alcohol *to excess* almost every time they try it. It's likely your kid will be reluctant to tell you the truth about their substance abuse because they have a fear of being reprimanded or grounded.

But if you've seen that your kid has issues with the law, issues at school and problems at home have started to become a regular occurrence, then they might just need my help. While my methods are effective with kids who are experimenting and kids who are abusing, my methods will probably sound a little drastic to the family of the kid who is experimenting. But how do you know if your kid is experimenting or abusing? Or to take it a step further, how do you know if your kid is experimenting and has the potential to begin abusing?

What is substance abuse?

In the 12-Step world of recovery, once a person starts using and cannot control the amount of a substance being used and cannot stop or avoid using, there's a problem. I know that is not what the Diagnostic and Statistical Manual of Disorders, 5th Edition (DSM-5) says, but I like things to be as simple and as direct as possible. Substance abuse is not just about using substances, but also how the substance affects one's life whether one is or isn't using a substance. Ask yourself: *Is my life or my kid's life unmanageable?*

An unmanageable lifestyle can be described as any of the following:

- Struggles at work or school or getting to work or school
- Issues with maintaining relationships with my friends and family
- Poor time management
- Delinquent financial maintenance or paying my bills on time
- Living an unhealthy lifestyle
- Poor hygiene
- Feelings of depression, anxiety, and uselessness

I work with families whose kids are tearing up the family and wreaking havoc in their own and their family members' lives, not the kid who is experimenting and can regulate their usage. As a parent, look for a change in your kid's social circles, their grades, their dating patterns, their sleep patterns, and any changes in their routine. These are some signs that all may not be well with your kid and that it is time for you to intervene and find out what has really been going on.

Don't always think your teenager is "just being a teenager."

Other things to keep an eye out for: trouble at school, trouble with the law, trouble with the family, and trouble at work. Too often, parents come into my office and think their kids are just being teenagers, and this might be true, but it can also be masking substance abuse. Somewhere in the past twenty or thirty years or so, binge drinking has become an acceptable phenomenon in high schools and colleges across the country. "It's just kids blowing off some steam, it's no big deal" is something I hear all too often.

Let's be totally clear, binge drinking is extremely dangerous, and it is a big deal. Just because your kid can get good grades or is polite at home but starts drinking Thursday or Friday night and keeps partying until Monday does not make them functional. The key ingredient here is the inability to control the amount that is being consumed. Alcoholics talk about how the real problem is the first drink, not the tenth. When you get hit by a train, it's not the caboose that kills you, it's the engine. Pay attention to your kid's drinking patterns, can they just have one beer or one drink or do they almost always get drunk? And remember, we are not talking about an adult that is drinking legally! If you are supplying the alcohol, you are liable for them and their actions, is that a risk that you are willing to take?

Here are some questions I ask parents who come to my office:

- What kind of substances might your kid be using? Alcohol, drugs, food, gambling, and porn all count as addictions. As addictions, they will be the primary focus of your kid's time and energy. For example, gaming, when it is an addiction, won't be a fun thing they do with free time, it will be a thing that keeps them out of class and causes them to avoid leaving their gaming system. Food won't be something that they eat because they get enjoyment and nourishment from it, it will be something that controls them, through calorie counting, restricted eating, or binging.

- What has the family already tried? Doctors, therapists, ministers, school counselors? I tend to be the last stop before they give up, so this list can be pretty long. Have you sought help for your kid before you picked up this book? If so, who have you turned for help? How many times? What have the responses been?

- Kids can be 14, 24, 34, or 44. Their age matters very little when you, as a parent, are worried about their wellbeing.

- The quickest way to find out if your kid is experimenting is to start testing them for drugs and alcohol and see how they react. Apply the consequences immediately and see how they respond.

If you think that this is your situation, then the course of action I suggest will make a lot of sense to you. If you are unsure whether or not this description fits your kid's behavior, then it is likely that the plan described in this book will seem harsh and unfair to you.

But if these descriptions match your situation perfectly, if you have tried everything and exhausted all of your options, then this may be the solution you have been looking for.

Key takeaways:

- Kids who are experimenting don't feel the need to continue experimenting with drugs or alcohol after they have been caught and experienced the consequences.

- Kids who are abusing cannot control the amount of a substance being used and cannot stop or avoid using. Often they show signs of trouble with the law, friends, family, school or work.

- It's critical to address the family system as a means to help the kid that is struggling with addiction and unmanageability.

- When a company is struggling, you address the management team first and then the employees, not the other way around.

- You are not responsible for your kid's addiction; you are responsible for how you react to it.

Chapter 3

Dear Parent: You Are In Control

As a parent, you likely feel one (or several) emotions: frustration, anger, or hopelessness. Your family members may be sitting around a table, blaming one another for what has gone wrong. And you may be thinking to yourself: *This is my fault. What did I do wrong?*

First, accept that this is not your fault. And second, know that you're not alone. It's not your fault that your kid likes to use drugs and alcohol. Kids grow more resourceful, so they will find whatever substances they want if they want them.

You can be the most loving, kind supportive parent on the planet and still end up dealing with your kid's substance abuse issues. And it is not a result of anything you have done wrong or right while raising them. It doesn't matter if your kid was breast-fed or bottle-fed, nurtured and given every opportunity available, addicts make up about 10 percent of the population.

Addiction is biological: if you have addiction in your family, you've got it. Similar to being pregnant, you either are or you aren't. And addiction isn't something that someone can pick up in a public restroom, or by hanging out with the "wrong crowd" or from watching too much MTV. Addicts come from all walks of life regardless of their faith, socio-economic background, education level, race, creed, color, and sexual orientation.

Your responsibility as a parent is how you react to the fact that your kid is using and abusing substances. Making significant improvements to your kid's life starts with setting up a system and addressing the way your family engages and interacts with each other, thus holding every family member accountable. Creating a family dynamic that has clear boundaries and expectations will allow you to deal with whatever adversity comes your way. Remember, you're not responsible for your kid's addiction but you are responsible for how you respond to it. You can learn to live with an addict that is active in their addiction or sober. You do not have to let them run the show with all the drama, crisis and chaos that comes with substance abuse.

I've been there. I've been a kid; I've been a parent, and I've been a family member of an addict. I have been an addict, myself. I have been the sober person who completed the steps, and I am a mental health professional who supports others as they face addiction. I understand all of the perspectives, so my recommended solutions are based upon my experience.

Consistency, accountability, and transparency are three critical elements of a successful resolution to drug abuse. And these components aren't just for the kid addict, but the parents as well.

To ensure these elements, setting boundaries, accountability measures, and structure are three important components to resolving your kid's addiction to drugs and alcohol. And your kid's addiction often has an effect on academics or behavior at home. This relationship between addictions and exterior behavior can take on different forms. Often a kid's academics and behavior at home may be fine, but partying is out of control. Or maybe your kid's academics aren't so great, while behavior at home hasn't been an issue, but the drugs and alcohol are the common threads. Any of these situations can lead to trouble for both you and your kid.

Boundaries

Start drawing lines. That's what a boundary is. The most important thing you as a parent can understand about boundaries is that boundaries aren't about your kid– they are about you. Boundaries are about you saying, "Enough!" and sticking to it.

Boundaries set parameters, letting the other person know what you will and will not tolerate. While we often use boundaries throughout our everyday lives, it is important to create and maintain a boundary with your kid. After all, you are still the parent in this situation, and both you and your kids need to understand and respect that dynamic.

An example of establishing boundaries with your kid can be any of the following:

- No using drugs or alcohol ever – in the house or with friends.
- No associating with friends or acquaintances in town that have a reputation for using drugs and drinking.
- In our house, we have the expectation of consistent attendance at school and maintaining a 3.0 GPA.
- In our family we do not use threats, hitting or yelling at each other and we use "please," "thank you" and "excuse me" when we are speaking to each other.

Accountability

Parents have often told me, "I have tried to set a boundary before, but my kid doesn't ever follow it." My question is always did you enforce any level of accountability? Accountability means you've established a consequence or counter-measure for activating that boundary if it isn't followed properly.

If a kid is drinking or using drugs and the parents told me, "We've told him no more drugs and alcohol, but he does it anyway," I would say, "Great. Let's start doing drug tests." But they will often respond with, "He knows how to beat them."

But your kid doesn't know how to beat a hair follicle test. Your kid can scam a urine test or a breathalyzer, but there is no way to trick a hair follicle test for drugs. And while you can use a breathalyzer on a consistent basis, kids might be able to fool it once or twice. But eventually, the tests will tell the truth.

While the cost of a drug test is always a factor, do remember that car accidents, therapeutic boarding schools, treatments, and funerals are even more expensive. You've created a boundary, now be accountable for it.

Boundaries without any accountability are a waste of time—both to you and your kid. For example, let's say that you are driving down the street. The boundary that's set for you is a speed limit of 35 miles per hour, but you speed past a cop, driving at 100 miles per hour. Rather than turning on his lights and immediately pulling you over, the cop just waves – there is no accountability! It doesn't matter if you broke the law, drove over the speed limit, and risked hurting yourself or anyone else. But if the cop is there with a radar gun to hold you accountable and you drive over the accepted limit, he will pull you over and give you a ticket. You need to hold your kids accountable in the same fashion.

What you are doing by setting boundaries and enforcing them through accountability and structure is the same thing. You are teaching your kids how to be adults, how to be responsible, and how to take responsibility for their behavior. These are often the biggest complaints that parents have about their kids: they don't have accountability or any level of responsibility.

Exactly. Because you don't hold your kid accountable. You take care of everything and allow your kid to make excuses for falling short or failing drug tests. Why should your kids show any level of responsibility for their actions?

Structure

If parents tell their kids to stay away from drugs and alcohol, but do not hold them accountable when they do dabble with drugs and alcohol, then the "No drugs and alcohol" boundary is meaningless.

For the teenager using drugs and alcohol, the parents can set the boundary: No drugs and alcohol. Then accountability comes when the parents explain that to enforce this rule, such as they will start breathalyzing their kid, along with administering weekly drug tests. The consistent structure is the final step to this regimen.

If the kid doesn't pass the drug test and shows positive results for drugs or alcohol, parents should then take away the kid's access to social life: computer and internet access, car and phone access, until they do pass the tests. Consistency is critical during this step of the regiment as success is created through repetition.

I'd be surprised to learn if your kid wasn't upset by this. At the extreme, your kid may run out the door at which a responsible parent can call the police and say, "I need to report my kid. He's gone. He's missing curfew, and we had this debate about drugs and alcohol."

The response I often get from parents at this suggestion is, "But then my kid will have a criminal record!" May I remind you: your kid might have a criminal record as a minor but the legal consequences are much less severe than when they're an adult. Occasionally, the cops will bring your kid home or ask you to come and pick him up. If your kid continues to cause this problem, your kid will end up getting a record, but at 18 years of age, that record will be sealed for your kid.

Wouldn't you rather your kid deal with addiction in the early teen years than at 18, 19, and 20 years old? At those older ages, an entirely different set of rules comes into play.

Situation analysis: Your kid has gone rogue

But what if your situation at home has gone to the extreme? Do you think your kid is going to literally run out of the house when your kid is no longer allowed to use the telephone, cars, and computers? Then we can discuss the next steps.

Understand that setting boundaries and holding a kid accountable is actually creating a safe environment for your kid. The fascinating thing is that kids often want and respond well to boundaries. Note that no kid wakes up thinking: *Wow, I wish my parents would hold me accountable and have more boundaries.*

But when there aren't any boundaries and there isn't any accountability, kids panic because there isn't any consistency.

I have seen family after family that begins holding boundaries around substance use, academics and behavior and the change that occurs are miraculous and almost immediate. Once kids know where the lines are and what the consequences are and that they will be applied consistently, they have a sense of predictability in their home and help them learn how to use these elements in their lives and create emotional regulation. Kids like their lives to be predictable; that makes them feel safe and allows them to grow emotionally and mature. When they don't know what will happen next, things can get really chaotic. The boundary you set is about saying to them, "I love you so much that I am not going to accept this behavior anymore. I am not going to tolerate this. This is not okay with me."

The most important part about boundaries is that they cannot be done punitively. Setting boundaries is not done with guilt, shame, finger-pointing, or arguing. It's done with love and compassion. An example you may say:

"Ben, I love you. I am no longer willing to accept your using drugs and alcohol. It's because I love you and I care about you. It's also not negotiable. It isn't a debate. I am telling you as your father that this is no longer acceptable. The way we are going to enforce is through consistent drug tests and breathalyzers. We will start by taking you to a facility and completing an initial drug test so that we have a baseline which will tell us which drugs you are using and how much you are using them."

It is critical to start with a baseline number for drug use so you can measure over time and see if they actually stop using or continue to use. And it sets the precedent with them that you are not making idle threats and that you mean business.

As I've mentioned before, I don't engage with the 16-year old drug users – I engage with the parents. After all, the change starts with the parents. I do encourage the parents to find a therapist for their kid and have some on my staff in Colorado that is amazing with adolescents, teens, and young adults. As a matter of fact, that's why I hired them!

Situation analysis: Disagreements among both parents

While I'll explain boundaries, accountability, and structure and parents will mention they've tried that approach before, I'll ask what happened when their kid-tested positive for drugs. The result I often hear, "We couldn't agree on what to do, and we weren't on the same page."

This is where the whole system can fall apart; if you don't take substance abuse seriously, then how can you expect your kid to? Write down what the boundaries are and what the accountability function is: No drug use and regular testing. Then, together, we move on to the third piece of this puzzle, which is the structure: if your kid tests positive for drugs, their devices, access, and social life will get taken away. The parents then always say the same thing: "We tried taking his phone, but he won't give it to us."

But, whose phone is it, actually? If your kid does not pay the bill, the phone belongs to you the parents. If you need to, you as a parent can reach out to your service provider and have the phone number removed from your plan or the service limited to only a few numbers and turn off the data plan, plus change the wireless password at the house. And you can always shut the phone off and get them an old fashioned flip phone. There is nothing more humiliating to a teenager than having a flip phone.

Devices can be tricky, and often require changing the Wi-Fi password to enforce. Most Wi-Fi providers have a router available that will allow you to shut down specific devices, and if you need to employ this, do so. When I say take away your kid's phone, I mean take away all of the electronics – the iPad, the PlayStation, the Xbox. All of those devices can access the internet. No TVs, no computers – take everything away.

Situation analysis: Your kid needs technology for schoolwork

What if your kid does their schoolwork on a computer (as most of them do now)? Have your kids complete their homework in front of you. While monitoring your kid's screen time, allocate a certain amount of time for your kid to complete homework, and if it's not done, then it's not done. That is your kid's fault and your kid's problem. Hold your kid accountable.

This leads to the second boundary with accountability and structure: the academics. Now, you are going to ask your kid's teachers for a weekly report on behavior and academics. Engage in emailing all of your kid's teachers, the principal, the school counselors, and the school psychologist. Tell them that your therapist said this is what you need to do, and that you need their help. It is generally very easy to get this put together. At this point, your kid becomes responsible for showing up at home on Friday afternoons with something from each of the teachers. This is either achieved or not: that is the structure. If it is not achieved, then your kid will spend the weekend doing their homework and chores. Once it is done, then you can start talking about some freedom.

Situation analysis: Should you incentivize good behavior?

I like things that are very tangible, so sometimes the incentive you offer your kid can be that they get to use their cell phone, get access to the internet, or get access to the car and social life. Those are three fantastic incentives, and ones that they will likely respond to. Another is that they get a social life.

If your kid can pass a drug test that you administer, keep up their academic progress, and behave well at home, they can have all of those things. Obviously, you want to continue to positively incentivize good behavior.

You can even choose to go long-term with your incentives and tell your kid, "If the drug test stays clean, you can get that GPA up to a 3.5, and you get your five hours a week of chores done, we would be open to this, this, and this."

At this point, I'm a big fan of bringing the kid into the conversation and asking, "What do you want?" They might say, "I want to get high," but that's not going to happen. It is never an incentive. Drugs and alcohol are never an acceptable incentive.

What if you feel uncomfortable with the idea of setting such strict boundaries for your kid? Then I suppose you need to ask yourself what, exactly, it is that you are doing here. I am very task and goal-oriented, as well as very direct and very straightforward. I will always ask my clients what their goal is. What is the goal with the drugs and alcohol? What's the goal with the academics? What's the goal at home? A lot of times, parents will say, "We've tried this before, but we can't get on the same page or the same team."

If you are uncomfortable with setting and reinforcing these boundaries, ask yourself a few questions: Do you not trust each other? Do you not rely on each other? What's the story?

Inevitably, one parent is being what we call a "helicopter parent," hovering over the kid and constantly taking care of things. If this is the case, usually the other parent is the drill sergeant. When this is the case, it is because this dynamic is usually familiar to how the parents were raised as well, so they are reacting to that and recreating an environment based on what they know and what they have seen.

Situation analysis: Deeper family dynamics

Deeper family dynamics and issues are often a key component of addiction. Once we arrest the behavior pattern of the kid, then we can work not just with the individual who is struggling with substances, but we can start talking about how the family is responding to the situation and why. We can start to dig in and do the interesting family of origin work with the parents and look to identify the history of substance abuse and mental health issues. We talk about what it was like in their household growing up and why they struggle with their ability to hold a kid accountable. Once we get our initial plan in place for drugs and alcohol, academics, and behavior at home, often a deeper family dynamic issue starts to come out.

Why aren't you able to hold your kid accountable? What's really going on there? Now, we are triaging the family. Everyone thinks we are triaging the addict, but really, we are triaging the whole family at once. When it comes to more personal issues, however, I generally refer clients to other therapists that are more engaged in processing than I am.

Key takeaways:

- You're not responsible for your kid's addiction but you are responsible for how you respond to it.
- Boundaries, accountability, and structure are three important components in resolving your kid's addiction to drugs and alcohol.
- Boundaries are about you, not your kid. You have to be willing to set them and hold them.
- Accountability is how you are going to hold the boundaries; what system of accountability are you going to use?
- The structure is a consequence or a reward for following the boundaries and accountability.
- Setting boundaries and holding your kids accountable is actually creating a safe environment for them.
- It's critical for both parents to agree on boundaries, accountability, and structure.

Here is a worksheet to get you started:

Boundaries

Drugs and Alcohol:

School or Work:

Behavior at home:

Accountability

Drugs and Alcohol:

School or Work:

Behavior at home:

Structure

Drugs and Alcohol:

School or Work:

Behavior at home:

Chapter 4

Getting Started: Create Plan A

By choosing this book, you realize your kid is not simply experimenting with drugs or alcohol, and actually needs help. While experimenting with drugs or alcohol is not necessarily acceptable, it is a common behavior among kids today. If you are one of the few lucky parents who have had their kids admit they have tried a few substances and didn't like them, and you are not seeing any significant changes in your kid's behavior or performance in school, then you likely don't need to follow the suggested recommendations outlined in the next few pages. (*Note that this chapter focuses on alcohol and marijuana. Please turn to Chapter 5 for a deeper focus on other harder drugs*).

In doubt about whether your teen has progressed beyond basic experimentation? Consider creating, implementing and sticking to a plan equipped with concrete boundaries, accountability, and structure.

One of the easiest ways to determine if a kid has progressed beyond basic and normal experimentation is by identifying changes in the kid's performance in school, social circle, and interest, such as after-school activities and sports.

The second easiest way is simply asking your kid to complete a drug test. As a general rule, people who are not abusing drugs or alcohol don't complain when asked to complete a drug test. But if your kid is using, expect your kid to complain, deny using drugs and attempt to find a way to beat the test and accuse you of not trusting them or not loving them.

You've set the boundary of "No drugs or alcohol." Now be accountable for it.

Holding a kid accountable to your "no drugs or alcohol" boundary starts with a drug test, either at a professional facility or at home. Choosing a twelve-panel drug test ensures comprehensive testing for as many drugs as possible.

If you're purchasing an at-home test, choose one that will test temperature, content and water level of urine. Testing temperature is important because if your kid is using someone else's urine to beat the test, it won't be warm. Testing the water level of urine is critical because drinking copious amounts of water just before a test can dilute urine.

One of the easiest ways to work around the test is by using someone else's urine, but a local testing facility has on-site professionals who will watch your kid take the test. And don't forget, you can also have your kid take multiple drug tests at random times and avoid telling your kid when he is going to receive a drug test, so there's minimal time for your kid to prepare for the test.

As an example, if you wake your kid at six in the morning, it's hard to prepare enough to fake the test. Or after an initial session at my office, I often tell parents to stop at the local pharmacy on the drive home, purchase a twelve-panel test and watch the kid urinate in the cup. Don't be shy about sitting in the bathroom and watching them fill the cup. But if this really bothers you, then take your kid to the local facility and have a professional handle it.

Regardless, if you believe your kid is trying to work around a urine drug test, skip to a hair follicle test at a local facility. A hair follicle test indicates drug or alcohol use up to 90 days prior to the test – and these tests are extremely accurate and impossible to cheat.

Several brands of hair follicle tests are available on Amazon and other online retailers. While a urine test will show immediate results, a hair follicle test will take more time. An advantage of visiting a local facility is that the team will provide results immediately, plus email the results in greater detail several days later. These results can indicate approximately how much and how often each drug has been used.

Do you think your kid is drinking? Purchase a breathalyzer and use it regularly. Test your kid before and after they come home or whenever you feel it is necessary. Basic breathalyzers are also available on Amazon for around $100. There is an amazing device called a Soberlink that looks like a mobile phone and takes a picture every time a person takes a test. The Soberlink can be set to go off multiple times a day and you cannot beat it. You either submit a positive or a negative test at the designated time or you don't and an alert is sent to whoever is monitoring the client.

Drug and alcohol testing can sound expensive, but a few hundred dollars spent on testing and intervening in your kid's addiction now is only a fraction of the cost of inpatient treatment, which can be up to $30,000 per month.

The results are in. Now what?

If your kid passes the drug test, allow your kid access to the phone, internet, social life, car and any other privileges that you, as a parent, are comfortable providing. But if your kid does not pass the drug test, enforce the consequences. Do not provide any privileges until your kid does pass the test.

What if the test results come back unclear? Refusal to take another test or unclear results is considered a positive result. After all, if someone is actively avoiding a drug test, it's likely they are trying to hide something.

Improve their performance at school

You've seen the test results, and now it's time to get your kid's performance at school back on track. It's unrealistic to demand perfection in your child, but it is realistic to expect good performance at school, meaning good attendance, good grades, and good behavior. Set clear expectations with your kid about what their job is right now: receiving a good education.

Once you have determined what your academic expectations are and shared them with your kid, start using boundaries, accountability, and structure.

Create a boundary for performance at school

Draw a firm line that your kid's GPA should be at a 3.0 or better. And integral to this boundary includes that your kid should not have any no missing assignments for any class and should have good attendance.

Accountability measures

Hold your kids accountable for meeting these boundaries by having your kids engage with their education. Stay abreast of performance through weekly reports from each teacher. Make your kids accountable for their education teaches responsibility.

Structure

If your kid is meeting your boundaries, they can have access to all privileges. If the boundaries are not achieved, show consistency and systematically remove their privileges, or remove all of them at once, if the performance is particularly bad.

Situation analysis: Learning disabilities or poor time management skills

If your kid is struggling due to a learning disability or poor time management, help them. Learn how your kid can receive support at school, such as a 504 or an IEP if your kid has a learning disability or social-emotional issues that prevent them from doing well.

If your kid is showing poor time management, ask your kid to show you what they're learning and how they problem-solve. It sounds time-consuming, right? It is, but you're a parent – and your kid is your top priority. Teaching your kid how to be a better student leads to success. Avoid completing homework for your kid or allowing them to blow off assignments. Time management skills are critical to career success, and teaching these skills starts now.

If your kid is struggling at school because of social or emotional issues, such as bullying or issues with their boyfriend or girlfriend, consider a therapist for your kid that specializes in working with kids at your kid's age. Sometimes kids turn to drugs and alcohol to self-medicate when they feel like they don't fit it or are being bullied, and a good therapist can help sort this out.

Tweak at-home behavior

Every family has different expectations or definitions of appropriate behavior at home, such as no foul language, no bullying, no violence, no property destruction, and completing chores on time.

What if, ultimately, you want your kid to show respect? You as a parent need to model this. If you expect your kids to be respectful, you need to be respectful of them and others, including your own parents. Kids learn by example, no matter how old they are, so provide them with an example of how you want to be treated. And modeling behavior goes for both good and bad behavior, so remember you are modeling what you would like to see from them.

Boundaries for at-home behavior

Setting boundaries at home can be fairly basic, such as no foul language, no bullying, no violence, no property damage, and having all chores done correctly and on time and speaking respectfully to all family members. Remember that these boundaries apply to everyone, not just your kids. If you want them to be respectful of you, then you need to lead by example.

Accountability for at-home behavior

Accountability can be as easy as starting a weekly family meeting to review everyone's behavior. But if you are unsure how to structure the discussion, start this process in a weekly family therapy session.

Structure for at-home behavior

If all of the boundaries are met (drugs/alcohol, school/work, and behavior at home), then all of your kid's privileges are restored. If the boundaries are not met, then remember consistency: restrict your kid's privileges until the next family meeting. Let your kid know that this is how you are going to handle things from here forward. No more arguing, fighting, bargaining or threats. You are going to host a simple meeting at the end of the week when everyone is going to review all the boundaries and see how it's going. Facts are facts, and kids cannot argue with drug tests, report cards from school and family meetings.

A common thread with developing a plan to stop your kid's addiction and improve the consequential performance at school and at-home behavior is to take action. After setting your boundaries, hold everyone involved accountable for their actions, including your other kids and yourself as parents.

Situation analysis: Your kid is playing the "I don't care" card

I've had parents tell me, "My kid says he doesn't care if we take away his phone and the internet."

Don't get caught up in playing a game of escalation with your kids. When you are arguing with a teenager, who do you think is winning the argument? The most important thing you can do for your kids is to show you love them by setting good boundaries and teaching them how to be responsible and accountable. Avoid arguing, shaming, bullying, threatening or raising your voice, but stick to a matter-of-fact conversation. After all, you are a parent and you set the rules.

As working professionals, the best managers in our lives are likely those who communicated very clear expectations, timelines and policies. These managers are supportive and want you to succeed, and if you're struggling with completing work quickly and efficiently, these managers will offer support to alleviate the situation.

This is exactly the kind of parent you want to be – like the best manager you ever had. Make your expectations clear and concise, always be available for support and advice, and remember that your job is to administer consequences and rewards. You want to be a parent, not your kid's best friend.

Situation analysis: It's convenient for *me* if my kid has a phone

Your kid may need a phone for your convenience, but your kid doesn't necessarily need a smartphone. Provide your kid with the old-fashioned flip-phone that doesn't have internet. Admittedly, parents have told me this works like a charm, as few kids would want to take a flip-phone out of their pocket for their friends to see. Your service providers can also set restrictions, such as time restrictions for when the phone will and will not operate and contact restrictions. A phone can be programmed to only allow calls to you or emergency services.

Restrictions can be applied to your internet access. It takes some creativity, but you can control what devices access your Wi-Fi, change your Wi-Fi password, or turn off Wi-Fi altogether. But if your child has homework that requires internet access, watch them do their homework or restrict the Wi-Fi access to a timeframe.

Restricting access to phones and Wi-Fi also includes other technologies, such as an iPad, tablet or Xbox. Are you nervous that you won't win a battle over physically taking the phone from your kid? Simply call your service provider to turn off the device and change the Wi-Fi password.

Removing access to the internet and phone quickly and effectively gives your kid a wake-up call. But the positive results and improvement in your kid's behavior won't occur if you as a parent don't stick to these actions.

Situation analysis: Should you incentivize good behavior? (Part Two)

It's important to positively incentivize good behavior. These incentives can be renewed access to their privileges, such as their car, phone, technologies, and social life. At this point, I'm a big fan of bringing the kid into the conversation and asking, "What do you want?" They might say, "I want to get high," but that's not going to happen. It is never an incentive. Drugs and alcohol are never an acceptable incentive. This is not a negotiation and getting high is never on the table as an incentive.

Timelines for improvement

Give your kid 30 days to show progress: drug tests are coming back with lower numbers or are close to being clean, better performance, including grades and attendance at school and positive behavior at home. Always reward improvement and effort by acknowledging your kid and their accomplishments

Thirty days is enough time to show improvement from a kid who is abusing alcohol and marijuana. But what if your kid is abusing stronger drugs - cocaine, heroin, opiates, methamphetamine or MDMA and benzodiazepines? Don't wait 30 days as death can be immediate. Jump to a different plan.

Key Takeaways:

- Hold your "No drugs or alcohol" boundary accountable with a drug test - either a urine test or a hair follicle test and a breathalyzer or a Soberlink.
- You are a parent and you set the rules.
- Set separate boundaries, accountability, and structure for behavior at home and behavior at school.
- If your kid needs a phone for your convenience, get them a flip phone until they follow your boundaries.
- If your kid is abusing alcohol and or marijuana, give them a 30-day window to clean up their act.
- Remember, when you are arguing with a teenager, who do you think is winning the argument?
- It's critical that you lead by example. What's good for the kid is good for everyone.

Chapter 5

Don't Give Up – There's a Plan B

You tried Plan A for 30 days, but your kid is still using drugs and alcohol, failing to meet your expectations at school and improve behavior at home. Or you skipped Plan A and need a new course of action because your kid has become involved with harder drugs that can cause death after just one use, such as heroin or cocaine. If this is the case, we need to implement a more immediate solution. Let's talk about what substance abuse treatment looks like and how to access it.

Your options for Plan B

Here's an overview of what the continuum of care looks like for substance abuse:

- **Medical detox facility**
  - Patients are monitored at all hours of the day and night by trained staff members to first get the drugs and alcohol out of their system and then medically stabilize them. This process can take anywhere from three to seven days, depending on the severity of the chemical dependency.
- **Residential treatment center (RTC),**
  - Commonly referred to as in-patient rehab, RTC programs start at a minimum of 21 days and can last up to 90 days, depending on the client and the severity of the case and the insurance reimbursement. RTC is not only for substance abuse abatement but also for establishing support groups and individual and group therapy and psychiatry. Patients can meet other patients who are becoming clean and participate in intensive programs designed to help patients figure out what to do when they are sober and leave the facility. Patients will also receive individual therapy, psychiatric sessions, group therapy, family therapy, experiential therapy, life skills sessions, and psychoeducation on a daily and weekly basis.
- **Partial hospitalization program, or a PHP**
  - Most patients complete an RTC and then go to the PHP level of care. These therapeutic programs tend to be at least 20 hours a week of programming and can include individual therapy, group therapy, psychiatric consultations, and life skills training

classes. Highly therapeutic, PHPs intend to help the patient resolve the reasons he or she uses substances and helps them work through it in a supportive environment. A PHP can last up to three months depending on the needs of the client. The goal of the PHP is to start the reintegration process from RTC back home. More often than not, PHP is done in conjunction with a sober living facility.

- **Intensive outpatient program (IOP)**
  - These programs are at least ten hours a week with the same programming as a PHP but usually allow the patient more time away from the program to get back to living at home, attending school, working if they have a job, and practicing the life skills they are hopefully learning from the program. IOPs still have a stringent set of rules and expcctations that the patient will not be late or miss a single appointment. At some facilities, their ability to complete the program depends on the patient's attendance. An IOP can last for three months or longer depending on the needs of the client.
- **Sober living home**
  - A sober living facility is a group house that is run by a sober house manager. The sober living houses have strict house rules and administer regular drug tests, but do not offer therapeutic programming other than regular house meetings and possibly a few mandatory 12-step meetings. The primary reason for the

lack of therapy is that it is expected that the patient will continue therapy and psychiatric consultation on their own time outside of the sober living house or they've engaged in PHP or IOP already and want to live in a sober environment. Sober living houses allow the patient to reintegrate into his or her previous life before detoxification while being surrounded and supported by others who are facing the same struggle. Sober living can last anywhere from three months to 12 months depending on the facility and the needs of the client.

It is recommended that six continuous months of treatment, 30 RTC and 15 days of extended care (PHP, IOP, OP, and sober living) are needed to effectively reverse the effects drugs and alcohol have on the body and the mind, while 24 months is recommended for those who have developed a severe opiate or benzodiazepine addiction. All statistics show that the longer a person stays in the continuum, the better their chances are of staying sober long term.

What next?

Now that implementing a more intense plan can resolve your family member's addiction, it's time to find an appropriate facility for them. No parent ever comes to this decision lightly, and few consider this option until it's a life-or-death crisis. Admittedly, it is hard to be proactive and take your time searching through all of your treatment program options when you are terrified your child may die from an overdose. This scenario often leads parents to make hasty decisions, and unfortunately, some treatment centers can implement shady business practices by preying upon families in this situation. But you can avoid this situation by understanding a few guidelines to consider when deciding to send your kid to an intensive rehab.

Rehab isn't cheap

Be honest about what you can afford. An RTC can cost $1,000 a day or more before insurance reimbursement and may not always be in-network with your insurance company. While it may be tempting to Google search "adolescent or teen treatment centers", you may likely find a list of places that have spent a lot of money on SEO and Google advertisements and may not actually be the best option. And for full transparency, beware of the people who leave a negative review of an RTC online, most likely they are the patients who hated being there and have not completed the program or did not stay sober. Contact the RTC directly and ask if you can speak with some families that they have worked with, I have found that these families will be very candid with you about their experiences. And you can ask your family therapist if they know of any addiction therapists in your town or if they have a list of in-state and out-of-state facilities. If you can't find answers to those questions, I have provided resources at the end of this chapter where you can find the appropriate treatment programs.

There are services that work with families to help them in this process. Educational consultants, treatment consultants, interventionists, family case managers and recovery coaches are some of the roles you may come in contact with during your search. All of them can provide excellent guidance for a family searching for the right treatment program for their child. It's important to screen these people to make sure that you are not being taken advantage of in a time of crisis.

Educational consultants specialize in working with families to help them determine their best treatment options. But there's a catch: these folks are expensive. Many consultants start at around $5,000. Good educational consultants will case manage the family and the addict, help the family find the right treatment center for the addict, and then act as a liaison while the addict is in treatment. If the addict needs extended care or a therapeutic boarding school, the consultant should be able to provide recommendations. Consultants typically have a relationship with each treatment center, extended care facility, and therapeutic boarding school, and have personally visited each facility to meet with the staff, review the grounds and determine if it's the right fit for their clients.

Educational consultants are incredible people who do fantastic work, but not every family can afford to hire one. If you do choose to hire an educational consultant, always ask the consultant if they are getting a commission from any of the places they are recommending. If they are, that may skew their recommendation and may not be the best choice for your child's treatment. It is critical to know if you are being steered into a facility for financial compensation, so ask ahead of time to ensure that this is not the case.

A good interventionist is worth their weight in gold. They can help guide the family through the process of finding an appropriate treatment program and having a hard discussion with their kid about going to treatment. And they can help the family make the plan for how to confront the addict and offer help. Most addiction therapists, psychiatrists and treatment programs will have an interventionist that they have worked with and can recommend. The cost can range from free to $25,000 depending on the level of services provided, remember that everything is negotiable. And ask for references and call them!

Aside from education consultants and interventionists, there are firms and agencies that specialize in family case management. These companies have relationships with treatment centers across the country and offer help with sober transportation, interventions, case management, choosing a treatment center and working with the family before, during and after the addict goes to treatment.

Family case management is a relatively new concept and comes with mixed reviews. Good case management comes with weekly contact with the family and the addict and can include planning for the intervention, working with the family while the addict is in treatment and helping the family plan for reintegration when treatment is over. A good case manager will have suggestions of resources for the family for therapy, support groups and reading materials to help them understand addiction and how it affects the family.

Yes, there are predators out there waiting for parents in crisis to jump on the first "nice-sounding" solution and accept giving any amount of money to keep their child alive. While the recovery business is very much a word-of-mouth reputation industry, it's critical that parents spend some time proactively looking for resources and avoiding a hasty decision. Ask everyone you talk to for references from other families that they have worked with and don't be shy about asking questions. This is your kid's life we are talking about and it's critical that you are direct and don't hold back when interviewing.

Set up your interviews

You have your lists of in-state options, out-of-state options, in-network facilities, and out-of-network facilities, or obtained one from your therapist or consultant or case manager. Now it's time to set up phone interviews or visit each facility or center in-person if you have the time. When speaking to the marketing representative at each RTC, request to speak with the clinical director, if possible. The clinical director should be able to tell you what the overall philosophy of the facility is and how they go about achieving success with their patients. They will also be able to tell you who they have the most success with, remember not all treatment centers are the same just as not all patients are the same.

This process of due diligence is about making sure you are finding the best fit. Ask the facility representative if they have a list of families who have used the facility in the past and are willing to share their experiences with you. It is also wise to ask the representative what issues families struggle with at their facility. Note that if the representative cannot answer that question honestly and directly, you should not be interested in that facility. You want a facility that caters to specific problems and issues.

Don't be shy about asking the facility representative if the facility has faced any issues in the past, such as legal problems. If they have given you a list of clients, ask the clients the same question. No facility is perfect, but it is important that you send your child to a place that will care for them and help them through fighting their addiction.

Some additional questions you should ask include:

- How long has the program been in business?
- Does the program hold accreditation with CARF, or the Joint Commission, and are they certified by LegitScript?
- Is the program licensed by the state to treat substance abuse disorders and mental health?
- Are there full-time, board-certified doctors on staff? How frequently can patients meet with doctors?
- Do the therapists have a master's degree or licenses? Do they have specialized substance use disorder (SUD) training?
- Does the program use data-informed, evidence-based therapies?
- Does the program incorporate family therapy in the treatment process?
- Is there a family program that you can attend while your kid is in treatment?
- Are treatment plans individualized for your kid's specific needs?

- Does the program offer dual diagnosis treatment? Can the program treat someone who struggles with addiction and a concurrent mental health condition? How do they accomplish this?

- Where do individuals live while in treatment and what level of supervision do they receive?

- How many individuals share a room?

- How long is the wait to get into treatment?

- Are the detoxification medications FDA approved?

- Can I use insurance to cover the cost of treatment? In-network or out of network benefits?

- What kind of support is offered after completing the program?

Doing your due diligence is critical in this step. Do not make a hasty decision out of panic or fatigue. Ask your trusted friends what they think. Meet others who are going through the same thing, and understand that you are not the only family to be dealing with this situation. Find out if it is possible for you to meet with other families who have had family members in the facility that you are considering, and listen to their experiences. Trust your instincts: if you think you are being hustled by a sweet-talking business development representative from a treatment center that has all the answers, then you probably are.

Ask your therapist for their input, and see if they know anyone else who would be willing to share their experiences with the facilities you are considering. This will require some paperwork and time, but it is worth it. And while you are doing all of this, try to avoid falling into the shame spiral of thinking: *What did we do wrong to make our child use drugs and need treatment?* There will be plenty of time for that after your kid is in treatment and while you continue with family therapy and your own individual therapy, but right now, focus on getting your kid the help needed as quickly as possible.

Don't be shy about finances with the treatment programs—they are all businesses that survive on referrals, and they need you just as much as you need them.

Everything is negotiable. Be open and honest with representatives about your situation. Some facilities have scholarship programs and financing options. Many times, you can find ways to work with the facility.

The importance of visiting the facility

If you have the time and funds to travel, it's a wise decision to visit the facility in advance and investigate the place. When visiting the facility, ask if you can see their programming for the week, the rooms patients stay, eat a meal and see what the dining facility looks like, and meet some of the staff members.

Some additional questions you can ask include:

- Do you have an exercise facility, equine therapy, art therapy, play therapy or trauma therapy?
- If so, then what kind is it? Can I talk to the therapists who will be providing these therapies?

- What is the philosophy of the clinical team?
- How did your team arrive at that perspective? Why?
- What is the expectation for family involvement? Is there a family program and weekly phone calls or therapy?

Note that a list of questions in the back of this book for you to take with you as a guide.

Some facilities offer wilderness programs. These are therapeutic treatment programs that offer 30, 60 and 90-day outdoor experiential programs where patients are required to learn how to take care of themselves, be part of a team, and be responsible to the group. These programs are very effective in helping kids mature, build self-confidence, and improve self-esteem. And the program connects children to one another and to the experience they are going through, without any of the distractions of the modern world. My clients and their kids have had wonderful experiences with wilderness programs, so it is worth considering this option.

Getting your kid to treatment

You've figured out your budget and your program, now how will you get your kid to the treatment facility, whether or not they're willing to go voluntarily? If they are willing to go on their own volition, then you're in luck. And this does actually happen, making the transition to the treatment center much smoother. Sometimes kids are aware of their substance abuse and actually welcome the opportunity to seek help. These kids will pack up their stuff and get in the car, knowing their life needs to change.

But what if your kid is not so thrilled with the idea of treatment or an extended wilderness experience? Talk to the treatment center about a sober transportation service, as this is how most individuals get to treatment.

If you choose this option, know what to expect. Two people will come to your house and meet with you ahead of time. They will organize when and where they are going to pick up your kid. Generally, this is done early in the morning at your house, and it should happen very quickly and efficiently. The sober escorts arrive at the assigned time, wake up your child, and let them know what's happening. They will give your kid a choice to pack a bag, or the escorts will pack one for them. After the bag is packed, your kid will have a chance to say goodbye. The sober escorts then either drive your kid to the airport or directly to the treatment program. This is always a hard experience for families. But remember: you are at the point of wanting to intervene with someone who is literally killing themselves with drugs and alcohol.

Although it may be hard to say goodbye to your kid and send them off to a treatment center, it is the only thing that you have left that you can do. It is important to choose the right facility and to know what to expect while your kid is in treatment. You will need to know what things will look like when they get out, and what they will have to do to continue on their new sober path. Letting go of them in order to allow them to receive help can be difficult. But it is necessary.

Situation analysis: My kid is over 18

Now, you may be asking, "What if my kid is over 18? What if my addict is my spouse or my sibling or my parent?" These are all great questions. I have used Plan A and Plan B with adults and I add Plan C. Plan C is if the addict is unwilling to go to follow Boundaries, Accountability, and Structure (Plan A) and they refuse to go to treatment (Plan B), then the family, spouse or siblings can let the adult addict know that until the substance abuse stops and the behavior changes, the addict is no longer welcome as part of the family. This is exactly what happened to me in 1991.

My family got help from some professionals that told them to set boundaries with me and let me know that in no uncertain terms until I quit drinking and using drugs, I was not welcome as part of the family anymore. It is critical that the whole family is in agreement before taking this tact. I recommend working with a therapist, a family case manager or an interventionist and making a plan and holding your line. My favorite statement to share with families is "We love you too much to keep watching you kill yourself."

One response I get from families where the adult addict is still living with them is: "If we kick them out, they will go live on the streets and kill themselves!"

My response is direct, "They are already killing themselves and you're facilitating it by allowing it to happen in your home. Why not offer them an alternative?" If the addict chooses to leave the home because they don't want to get sober, then tell them you love them and will respect their choices but they cannot continue to live at home and use. Every time they call or text, you should respond with the same message, "We love you and want you to get help. Are you ready to quit using?"

The alternative is to allow the addict to keep dying a slow death in the home and have that affect the entire family. This is not the old "tough love" approach of locking them out and turning your back on them. This approach is about telling the addict that you love them and will do anything to help them get help if they are ready. But until they are ready, you need to set a firm boundary. It has been my experience personally and professionally that this is the approach that works. Sometimes, it takes weeks or months for the addict to test the boundaries and eventually see that the family means business.

Key takeaways:

- The continuum of care starts with detox, RTC, PHP, IOP, and sober living homes. Choose the one that's right for you and your kid.
- Your family therapist may be the best resource for choosing a treatment option.
- Don't be afraid to ask to speak with other families that have been through this process before you.
- Do your research before picking a treatment facility and don't be afraid to ask questions.

- You can engage an educational consultant or a family case manager in the process of picking treatment options. Make sure you ask them for references.

- If you have the time, try to visit some of the programs that you are considering.

- If the addict is over 18 or is an adult, you can still use Plan C, if they refuse Plans A & B.

Chapter 6

Your Kid Is In a Treatment Facility – Now Take a Breath

One of the most common questions my clients ask is, "My kid is in treatment, so what do I do now?"

One of the saddest, yet common things about this process is that once a kid is in treatment, the family becomes invisible until the week before their kid comes home. Acting this way is as if you're dropping off a kid at Best Buy, telling the salesperson your kid is broken and you will be back in 60 days to pick up the replacement. Junior is in treatment, the problem is solved, so all is good, right?

A parent cannot expect their kid to do something the parent is not willing to do as well. When an addict begins treatment and recovery, then the family must follow likewise. Note that the family will not necessarily have to go to treatment, but there are treatment centers that specialize in working through codependency and family of origin trauma and issues and are noteworthy options for a family with multiple issues that need to be addressed.

Codependency is a common concurrent theme in families with addiction, and it easily becomes an issue for all family members. When parents become codependent on handling the kid with an addiction, it is often detrimental to the other kids or family members in the house, causing significant problems and trauma for everyone involved. Additionally, the addicted kid becomes the focus of the family, and this masks deeper issues within the family or marriage. Getting an addict to treatment is just the first step; there's a larger recovery process for the family that must take place. So take a breath: your kid is safe in his treatment facility. Now let's look at the larger family ecosystem.

Ideally, families engage in family therapy and individual therapy at least once every week. And it is always wise to attend therapy sessions at the treatment center if possible, so parents and treatment specialists can together create a plan for when the kid returns home. Rarely do kids who go to treatment come from families that don't have some larger issues behind or in tandem with the addiction.

The 30 to 90 days a kid is away in treatment is the best time for the family to start their own healing process as it is easier to analyze what happened that could have contributed to the kid's addiction, work out solutions and restructure the family environment while the kid is safe and away at a treatment facility. During this time, family members stop blaming each other for what went wrong, work together on repairing the family dynamic and open up about individual issues.

I have often met with parents of addicts who told me, "There is no addiction or mental health issues in our family other than this one person. No generational issues either. We have no idea how this happened!"

While I used to believe these families were lying to me to cover up some deep, dark secrets, in reality, many families don't actually see their own larger issues. Let's be honest. No one wants to admit that they have addictions or mental health issues because society shames, ostracizes or simply views people differently. But every family has something: I have never met a family that doesn't have something in the family tree that needs to be addressed.

Behaviors that families often need to work on

I often hear: "I am not the one with the problem, why do I have to go to therapy?"

The answer? Addiction is a family disease. And it affects everyone who is engaged with the addict. Some of the traditional family behaviors that must be addressed during recovery include keeping secrets, blaming others, ignoring the addiction, normalizing the addiction and pretending as though nothing has happened.

Keeping secrets

Keeping secrets is all about dysfunctional ideas of loyalty. My friend Sarah called me one day to tell me that one of her kid's friends drank too much to the point that the friend had to be carried out of parties and driven home. Sarah's daughter didn't want Sarah to say anything to the friend's mother, so Sarah asked me what I thought she should do.

I asked her, "If it was your daughter, would you want to find out that everyone else knew about her drinking and never told you?" Even further, I asked Sarah to envision a scenario in which the friend's daughter ended up in an accident or died, so how would she feel facing the girl's parents, knowing she had never said anything to them before.

It's easy to hide behind the thought that it isn't someone's place to say anything because it doesn't involve their kid. But we say in the world of recovery: we are only as sick as our secrets. Real friends tell the truth to each other and are not afraid to risk a few hurt feelings. If someone could potentially be hurt or is hurting others, it's wise to speak up.

Another level of secret-keeping is in the family itself. It's not unheard of for a family to have skeletons in the closet that are kept hidden from the younger generations. This is done for a number of reasons and none of them are healthy. More often than not, the family has learned to keep the skeletons hidden due to the shame that the story brings to the family. This is the old "What would people say?" syndrome. The rationale is that it is best to keep the skeletons hidden and present the prettiest front forward and act as if there are no skeletons. In my business, we call this denial.

The next excuse is "It is no one else's business", and this is driven by the same shame of "We don't want the neighbors to know because then what will they think of us?"

And my favorite excuse I've heard is: "Well that was so long ago, I didn't think it was relevant to today."

This is all about hiding the skeleton way in the back of the closet and acting as if nothing ever happened and if it did happen, then it is not really relevant to what we are dealing with today. This is just not so! Everything is relevant to the current situation. Addiction and codependency are generational family issues that have ripple effects and create traits that are passed down from generation to generation.

The blame game

The blame game can start pretty quickly among individuals who prefer keeping secrets and often sound something like, "Well if you think my kid is bad, you should hear what people say about your kid!"

This is just a defensive comment. A person can always sit down with the friend and explain, "Look, none of our kids are perfect, and none of us are perfect, but I am concerned about your kid. If I were you, I would want to know. If you need help, please let me know. We are all in this together."

This is a lot more effective than gossip and brings the focus back to family, friendship and community. Blaming others is a deflective and defensive act because you then behave as if you are the victim and someone else is at fault. By doing this, you are removing the responsibility of the situation from yourself and placing it on someone else. In this way, you are absolving yourself of taking active steps to prevent or change it. If you are not at fault, it is not your job to do the work to change.

Accepting responsibility

Addressing a family's addiction issues means that all family members understand the individual role they play in it. Not once has a parent visited my office and been entirely surprised by their kid's substance use and abuse. In each scenario, the parent always knew about it, though it was no big deal or believed the other parent was addressing the issue.

When this happens, the blame game begins. The substance abuse becomes the school's fault, the coach's fault, the friend's fault or the girlfriend's fault. But if your kid is making poor choices in friends, activities and the people they are dating, it is your responsibility to parent them around this, not tell yourself or act as though you are helpless to stop it. While you cannot bully your kid into making good decisions, you can counsel and advise them. Use boundaries, accountability, and structure on their behavior.

Boundary

If you don't like the people your kid has been hanging out with, set a firm boundary with them. Make it very clear there will be no hanging out with kids who are using drugs and alcohol.

Accountability

Instruct your kid to account for their time, answer the phone when you text or call, and that you will be giving random drug tests to ensure your kid is not using substances with friends.

Structure

If your kid cannot or will not account for her time, ignores you if you call or text, or does not submit to random drug testing, you will remove privileges.

View this as an opportunity to talk and listen to your kid. Don't lecture; instead, say that you are concerned about your kid's choices and want to know what's going on. Ask your kid about their friends and be available to your kid on your kid's terms, talk about what your kid wants to talk about, and listen to your kid.

Learning to listen

One of the biggest parenting mistakes I see repeatedly in my practice is that parents won't listen when a kid is telling them about their lives. Instead, the parents are already forming opinions and judgments about their actions. And most often, a child will stop sharing information. Consider the Speaker-Listener method (see appendix explaining this method). Overall, the speaker talks and the listener listens and then repeats what the speaker says back to them. This is not an opportunity to prove that you are right and they are wrong; this is a chance to listen and connect.

Kids are always telling me that they talk to their parents, but the parents just don't listen to them or hear what they are saying. I have watched so many adults with their kids and I can see what they're doing. Instead of listening, they're formulating their response or their argument to show how they are right and their kid is wrong. One of the most important things a parent can do is listen to their kids and acknowledge their feelings and emotions. Listening doesn't mean agreeing or conceding a point - it's just an act of respect.

Normalizing poor behavior

Ignoring and normalizing substance abuse another common behavior among families with addiction. I often hear statements such as, "All of the other kids drink and use drugs; it's no big deal" or "You drink and used pot, you told me you did when you were my age, don't be a hypocrite!"

It's okay to be a hypocrite in this situation. Just because you, the parent, drank or used drugs, it does not make it okay for your kid to do the same thing. If your kid has a substance abuse issue, then you may want to consider your own drinking and drug use, not necessarily because you have a problem, but because it is hard to look at your kid and tell them to stop when you are not willing to do the same thing.

It is a sign of support to tell your kid who is in treatment that you are willing to support them by looking at your own personal drinking and drug use. This move is all about showing your kid that they are not in this alone. And this is an act of support and love. Creating an atmosphere of honesty and vulnerability in the family is the antidote for all of the negative byproducts of substance abuse.

You do not have to accept that your kid drinks or uses drugs and that these things are necessary for them to fit in or to have a social life.

Working on codependency

All of the behaviors listed above: keeping secrets, refusing to accept responsibility and allowing your kid to determine their own behavior, are all acts of codependency. Other actions can also contribute to this unhealthy dynamic, such as providing kids with financial assistance to keep them from getting into more trouble, backing down when addict behaviors happening, and making excuses for a kid's behavior are all symptoms of codependency.

I have listed books in the last chapter of this book that I encourage all parents of kids with addiction to reading. More than a few of them center around codependency: what it looks like, how to recognize it in yourself and others, and what to do to break the cycle of codependent behavior so that you and your kid can move forward together in a healthier, happier and more supportive sober environment.

Key takeaways:

- Codependency is a common concurrent theme in families with addiction, and it easily becomes an issue for all family members.
- Some of the traditional family behaviors that must be addressed during recovery include keeping secrets, blaming others, ignoring the addiction, normalizing the addiction and pretending as though nothing has happened.

- Just because the addict is in treatment doesn't mean everything is okay. That's just the first step in healing the family.

- You cannot expect your kid to succeed after treatment if the family system has not changed.

Chapter 7

Reintroducing Your Kid Back into the World

Whether you have followed Plan A and your kid has found success, or you have gone through the struggle of Plan B and your kid is out of rehab, what can you do to help them stay focused on their sobriety? What resources might be out there that can help both you and your kid along this new path?

One of the most important lessons to take away from this book and your recent experience is that you, as a parent, should never expect your kid to do something you would be unwilling to do. As a parent, provide your kid with an example of the type of behavior you would like to see from him. For example, if you would like your kid to attend regular therapy sessions, you should also make an appointment with a therapist. If your goal is to have your kid attend 12 Step meetings in your area, make sure you are attending meetings meant for the families and addressing their issues.

Aside from setting an example for your kid, additional follow-up methods can also assist you in learning what the next span of time might look like for you and for your teen. Being clean and staying sober are new experiences for an addict. Often, the addiction has kept them from facing reality and their issues, and now there is no buffer between them and their problems. In some cases, this shock to the system can lead to relapse for an addict and a fallback into old, familiar patterns for their families.

Avoid old patterns and behaviors

How do you avoid these? It starts with seeking both individual and family therapy for you and your teen. Include everyone who lives in your household in these family sessions, as they have experienced living with and loving an addict and they will likely need some guidance about what to do next.

Just because the addict is now clean and sober does not mean that the problem has been solved and everything will now be "normal." All "being clean" means is that the crisis you all faced together is now over. Now, it is time for you all to address the family patterns that you have become comfortable with and learn how to change them, in order to move forward. Old patterns will no longer apply, so learning new ways to deal with stress, difficulty, static amongst family members and any other problems that may arise will be keys to success.

Make sure that whatever therapy model and therapist you choose fully addresses both the addiction your teen went through and the codependency you, as their parent, experienced. Spend some time getting to know your provider to determine whether they are the ones for you. Make sure they are knowledgeable about both addiction and codependency. Ask them about the method of recovery you and your teen have chosen, and ensure that they are well-versed in it.

The worst thing parents can do when they are dealing with a newly clean addict is to bring them back into a family dynamic that has not changed. Your kid's reasons for using drugs or alcohol may stem from the home. And in many instances, this is true. If the home does not change, then nor will the urge to use. If the family system does not go through an overhaul after the upheaval of implementing Plan A or Plan B, you will more than likely find yourself back in the same crisis you were in when you picked up this book. Avoid this recipe for disaster by doing the legwork and getting yourself, your child, and your family familiar with the difficult work that lies ahead.

Most of the families who find success when they work with me are the ones who are willing to do the hard work of continuing to grow, evolve, and change their behaviors and patterns after their kid leaves the rehabilitation center or halfway house. They are willing to read all of the books I suggest to them when we are working together. The books I recommend deal with both of the problems: addiction and codependency.

These successful families are also willing to continue working in a therapeutic environment, both on their own, with their kid who is now in recovery, and with the other members of their family who have also been affected by the addiction. The addicts, themselves, make the decision and commitment to attend AA, NA, or CA or another support group meeting, while their families find their own support meetings, such as ACA, Al-Anon, Codependency Anonymous, and attend with as much regularity as the addict.

Each individual involved is willing to work the steps or engage in a spiritual practice that helps them to change their behaviors. These spiritual practices change from person to person, depending on their faith and what they feel the most comfortable with, and can range from taking yoga classes and learning to meditate to finding a spiritually-based group and connecting with the message and people in it.

Stick with it

For both the addict and the codependent, I have two conditions they need to meet before they move forward with other forms of therapy and addiction management (such as therapy or AA). The first is that the addiction and the family disease must be under control. Neither behavior can change if it has not reached a full stop first. When someone stops drinking, for example, they do not do so by slowly pouring half an ounce less into their glass over time. To quit a behavior as ingrained as addiction or codependency, it must first stop being the only behavior that either party knows.

Secondly, the behavior must change. As it turns out, this is usually the hardest part, which can come as a surprise to some people who have gone through the difficult, sometimes agonizing process of implementing all of Plan B. However, it can be easier to change certain things about ourselves when we are in an environment designed to help us stick to the commitment made to change it, such as a treatment center. Designed to turn people away from using, there is 24-hour around the clock support with days and nights highly structured, leaving little room for downtime, boredom, or dwelling on negative or traumatic experiences.

When these environments no longer surround an addict, the urge to use can potentially become overwhelming. For this reason, no one is kidding when they say the road to recovery is a long one. It requires regular work and effort on the part of everyone involved, and that work only occasionally becomes easier with time. When you become involved in the next steps of recovery, it is imperative that you and your kid commit yourselves fully to the process and stick with it, even when it seems like everything is going swimmingly.

Some books and videos I recommend

When parents are looking for more information outside of our sessions that may help them move forward with and understand their kid better, I often recommend specific books to them that may help them work through their situation and gain greater insight and understanding into what has been going on in the home.

I am personally a huge advocate of the work of Brene Brown, and I recommend her to all of my clients. She is a research professor at the University of Houston and specializes in studying empathy, courage, shame, and vulnerability. Her stance is that we all must "walk through vulnerability to get to courage," and her viewpoint on vulnerability is refreshing and honest.

I highly suggest at least one viewing of her TED Talk on vulnerability (2010) and shame (2012). Both of these can be found online through her website, as well as on Amazon. I also recommend all of her books, beginning with *Daring Greatly*. Additionally, you can visit her website and find a therapist who utilizes her work, if you find that what she has to say resonates with you and your child while you are traveling along the road to recovery.

I always believe that every family and addict can benefit from watching Pleasure Unwoven, an amazing documentary by Dr. Kevin McCauley. Dr. McCauley explains the biological side of addiction and implements a 10-point plan for recovery that is fundamental for both the addict and the family and he shares his own experiences with his addiction. His second documentary, Memo to Self, is as good as the Pleasure Unwoven and I think that both should be mandatory.

A book I cannot recommend often enough is *Parenting Teens with Love and Logic*, by Foster Kline, M.D., and Jim Fay. This book was written to help parents prepare their teenagers for what responsible adulthood will be like, and can often be a boon for those parents who feel as though they are underwater when it comes to giving their teen the guidance that they know they need. The goal of the book is to give parents the empowerment they need to set boundaries, impart necessary skills, and encourage positive decision-making skills in their teenager. Topics the authors cover include ADD, divorce, and addiction, making it a great addition to the family library.

Codependent No More, written by Melanie Beattie, is a gold-standard in self-help and recovery circles. Because so many clients of mine face the issue of codependency alongside their teen's addiction, I generally steer them towards this book, so they can understand why and how this codependency happened and what they can do about it from here on out. Beattie gives readers self-assessment tests and exercises, so they can apply the things they are learning to their own situations. The guidance this book provides is laid out well and is easy to follow, making it a great tool for parents to utilize as they try to fix the codependency that they have developed. She has an updated version, *The New Codependency*, which helps people understand that they don't have to have an active addict in their lives to be suffering from codependency, sometimes dealing with mental health issues or generational trauma can create dysfunctional family patterns as well.

Along the lines of codependency in parents, *Facing Codependence: What It Is, Where It Comes from, How It Sabotages Our Lives* is another great read that can really open the eyes of parents who need a gentle push into understanding how things in their family have unraveled because of codependency. The author, Pia Mellody, gives parents a solid framework for identifying and understanding codependent thinking, behavior, and feelings, as well as a clear list of what codependency looks like. It also gives a lot of insight into what might have started the codependency that a parent can experience, which can go a long way towards breaking the pattern of it.

Alcoholics Anonymous and *Paths to Recovery* are both incredibly useful resources for both parents and addicts. Both address the AA and Al-Anon steps, concepts, and traditions, which can be a great way for parents and teens to both find some help of their own and also read something that gives them insight into what the other is doing and working on. These books are ones I almost always recommend as companion reads for families who are committed to attending meetings.

In the Realm of Hungry Ghosts, by Dr. Gabor Mate, is a great choice of book for anyone who is dealing with addiction, either their own or their child's. The true stories of the things other people have experienced give a good representation of the people who can be affected by addiction. Spoiler alert: it's everyone. It's a useful book to help people understand that addiction is something that can happen to anyone, at any time.

Lastly, I always recommend that clients take a look at a particular landmark study: https://www.cdc.gov/violenceprevention/acestudy/ about adverse childhood experiences. The website belongs to the CDC, and there are links to click through explaining the study itself, resources to use to understand the study and the results, and articles that cover a broad range of topics about adverse childhood experiences. This study gives a lot of insight into how things that happen to individuals as children can affect their behavior later in life. It's an incredibly useful study, and I strongly encourage clients to read it to gain more insight into how these types of experiences end up shaping us as teenagers and adults.

Key takeaways:

- The worst thing parents can do when they are dealing with a newly clean addict is to bring them back into a family dynamic that has not changed.
- Happy families come from happy individuals; everyone should be addressing their issues in therapy and 12 step support groups.
- There are lots of great books about families and addiction available, don't fall into the trap that once the addict is sober everything is all better.
- Consistency, Accountability, and Transparency are critical in the sober person's and the family's success.
- Make a plan for when your kid comes home that includes family therapy, individual therapy, and support groups for everyone, and having fun together as a family.

Chapter 8

Resources to Continue Your Journey

Once you and your family have completed Plan A or Plan B, one of the best things that you can do is have an ongoing commitment to follow-through. What does follow-through mean? Ongoing individual and family therapy among you, your family and your kid to continue working through the reasons the addict in your family may have used. This ongoing therapy can also mean introducing both your kid and you to a group of supportive individuals who can understand the struggle of staying clean.

For hundreds of thousands of addicts throughout the country, support groups give them a place to be honest, to feel welcomed, to talk about their difficulties without judgment, and to find others who have been or currently are going through the same experiences.

A number of options and resources are available for both you and your child. You can spend some time on the internet, researching each option, and from there, decide which ones may be best for you and your kid. Additionally, ask your kid what they would find the most helpful and be most comfortable with using will help you narrow down your choices and find the right fit. The best thing I can recommend is that you go to meetings, meet the therapists, read books, watch videos and engage in the recovery communities and see where you fit in. The internet is great for making lists and getting directions but I have worked with too many people that look at a website and find some small trivial reason that keeps them from actually participating or going to an event and getting involved. There is no substitute for direct human contact with other people fighting the same battle as you.

Ask your therapist and your kid's therapist about groups recommended for people who have found themselves in your situation. Your therapist will likely have significant knowledge of the best support groups in your area for your particular situation and can give you recommendations based on their experience with you and your family. Many groups will have several day and time choices for meetings, so you can also try out a few different groups in your area to find one that will provide you and your kid with the most support. If you cannot find anything in your area, contact us and we will help you find some.

Conclusion

Congratulations on finishing the book. I hope my journey has helped you and given you some vision on what do to next with your family. My goal was to write a book that described what its like to be in a session with me. I want to share my experience of being a member of an addicted family, an addict, getting sober and working in the mental health field with families like yours. Addiction isn't leaving us any time and I know that there are more people out there looking for help than I can possibly reach in my lifetime. And I also know that my plan doesn't work for everyone, I know it worked for me and has worked for my clients and their families.

I know I sound like a broken record but its imperative to reiterate that you cannot expect an addict to do something you are not willing to do. If you want them to get into recovery, then you need to recover as well. Families always ask me, "What can I do to support my kid/sibling/spouse/loved one?" and my answer is always the same, "The best thing you can do is get into your own recovery and change your life." Nothing has a greater impact on a family system than one person changing the way they live. Don't preach or try and fix anyone else, just take care of you and set strong boundaries and hold them. The impact of one person in recovery on a family is nothing short of a miracle, everyone has to acknowledge that the family system has changed. Once the train has left the station, you cannot back it up and act like nothing happened.

I hope that my personal story helps you to understand that I am not writing this from an intellectual or academic perspective, this is my real life experience. I think that is what makes me an effective therapist with my client families. I can look them in the eyes and they can tell that I have been down this road before and I have a solution to offer them. And if they don't want my help, I am not offended, I hope and pray that they find what they are looking for. I have had many families meet with me once or twice and decide to look elsewhere for support. I will say that a lot of them come back six months or a year later and say, "You were right, it didn't get better, it got worse." I don't gloat or feel superior, I let them know that the plan is the same as it was when we met before; try Plan A for 30 days and see how it goes, if the kid can quit or moderate, good for them, if not then go to Plan B and if they're over 18 and not willing to go to treatment then go to Plan C. Remember that consistency, accountability and transparency are the keys to both recovery from addiction and codependency. Don't try to do it alone, get qualified help and ask lots of questions. If you can't find anyone in your neighborhood, send us an email and we will be happy to point you in the right direction.

The last thing I want to tell you is that you are not alone. Families like yours are dealing with addiction and codependency every day and they're at your gym, your church, your office, your kid's schools. One of the most frustrating parts for me as a therapist and an addict in recovery is how long it takes people to ask for help. This is almost always driven by secrets and shame, I know it was in my house and we had no idea what to do or where to go for help. If this book does nothing else I hope it helps families find resources and start a conversation.

Kevin Petersen, MA, LMFT

Petersen Family Counseling

www.petersenfamilycounseling.com

Resources for you and your family

Al-Anon www.alanon.org

Al-Anon may be one of the most recognized and widely used support group services in the country. The website has an FAQ section that you can browse if you are not sure what you are looking for or what going to a meeting may look like. Al-Anon is not for alcoholics; it is designed as a support system for those who are in the same situation that you find yourself in: they are the family and friends of alcoholics. The focus of Al-Anon rests on helping to deal with and solve the most common problems that families of those with an addiction to alcohol often face.

It is important to note that at Al-Anon meetings, the alcoholic is generally not included. It can be easier for the families of alcoholics to speak freely about their experiences without the addict there, so they will have separate meetings and support groups of their own.

Al-Anon is for the family of an alcoholic, not an addict or alcoholic, specifically. Please also note that the primary individuals who attend Al-Anon meetings are those who have a family member or friend who is an alcoholic, not a drug addict. If your child's problem revolves around drug use, you may find Nar-Anon more helpful.

Nar-Anon www.nar-anon.org

Nar-Anon, like Al-Anon, consists of group meetings for the families and friends of addicts. The Nar-Anon program consists of twelve steps, like NA or AA, and bases its program off of those. Again, like any of the other "Anonymous" meetings, there are no fees to pay or rules for joining; you and your family simply attend a group in order to participate. If your child has had a drug problem, Nar-Anon may be your best bet to find support in your community. The website will have lists of meeting times and places in your area, you can look for the organization in the white pages, or you can simply search online to find a meeting close by. If there is no Nar-Anon group in your area, the website will allow you to click through a link to start one.

Adult Children of Alcoholics (ACA) www.adultchildren.org

If you have other kids, particularly older ones, who have been affected by drinking in your family, this is a great resource for them. Often, parents may figure out, through their struggle with their child who uses drugs or abuses alcohol, that they may have a problem, themselves, or that they may be the child of an alcoholic and have not been aware of it until now.

ACA can be a tremendous resource for individuals who find themselves in this situation. As adults, many people process the events of their childhood differently than they would if they were kids, and they can also learn to recognize behaviors that they engage in because their parents were alcoholics and they may not have known it. Additionally, growing up in an alcoholic household can do lasting damage to relationships with others, and part of the healing process can be working through those issues in a safe and supportive environment. If this sounds familiar to you, ACA may be a good choice. Once again, visit their website for meeting times and places in your area, or learn how to start one yourself.

SMART Recovery https://www.smartrecovery.org

Families Anonymous https://www.familiesanonymous.org

Resources for your kid

Having covered a few of the best resources for you and your family while you go through the hard work of moving forward from your kid's alcoholism or addiction, now it's time to go over a few of the things your child may find the most helpful. These resources will be particularly helpful if your child has spent time in a rehabilitation or treatment center, or lived in a group home or halfway house, as many times those environments implement many of the techniques used in these resources.

Alcoholics Anonymous (AA) www.aa.org

Probably the most well-known resource worldwide for those who struggle with alcohol addiction and dependence, AA is the most likely place for your child to start if they have had a drinking problem. AA meetings are often widely attended and can have specific markers for attendance, such as meetings for men, meetings for women, and meetings for teenagers. There are usually several meetings a day in most metropolitan areas, and they are held at a variety of locations.

AA will provide your kid with a support system of individuals who have faced or are facing an addiction to alcohol. Your child simply has to attend to take part, and there are no fees or charges. At a meeting, your child will meet a sponsor, someone to whom they can talk if they are feeling the urge to drink or even just having a hard time. The program is run based on the twelve-step system. Many people attend AA meetings for most or all of their lives, even if they are not currently drinking, because of the support the meetings can provide on the road to and during sobriety.

Narcotics Anonymous (NA) www.na.org

NA, like AA, is a widely used resource for those struggling with addiction and it has become more frequent over recent years, due to the increasing availability of narcotics and the uptick in users all over the country. Like AA, there are many options for meetings, and you will likely find one in your area that will meet the needs of your kid the best. The foundations of NA are also similar and use the twelve-step system to work through the addict's issues. NA is a program that requires complete abstinence from all drugs, so it is important that your kid understands that they cannot attend these meetings if they are using it at all.

Cocaine Anonymous (CA) www.ca.org

Another option in the twelve-step recovery system is Cocaine Anonymous (CA), so if your kid's drug problem has revolved around cocaine or any other drugs, you may want to send them to these meetings, instead of AA or NA. They use the same book and 12 steps as Alcoholics Anonymous.

SMART Recovery www.smartrecovery.org

SMART Recovery is an alternative to NA or AA, for those who do not find these programs helpful. SMART Recovery is a four-point program that utilizes a science-based system to help your child maintain sobriety. The program avoids the use of words such as "addict" or "alcoholic", so if you find that your child struggles with these particular labels, this may be an option for them. SMART is based around the idea that using alcohol and drugs is a way to cope with problems and emotional upsets but can become problematic when drinking or drug use becomes heavy or out of control. The SMART program focuses on research-based techniques to help your kids work through their daily life after they are sober and learn to deal with problems that they may face as they arise.

Generally speaking, SMART Recovery does not focus on past experiences as much as NA or AA does. If your kid finds that that setup does not work for them, they may want to give SMART a try. There are no sponsors in SMART Recovery; instead, the meetings are run by facilitators, some of whom are professionals or who have had issues with drugs or alcohol in the past, some of whom have not. While the program at SMART Recovery meetings differs from that of NA or AA meetings, many individuals attend both and can find both helpful for different reasons.

While SMART is not a spin-off of the "Anonymous" program, the two can be used concurrently if your child finds that they are helpful.

Also note that SMART Recovery offers meetings and programs for friends and families of addicts and alcoholics, as well as ones that are based around any court-ordered support group participation, and they also have meetings designed specifically for teenagers and younger people.

Celebrate Recovery www.celebraterecovery.com

Celebrate Recovery is similar to NA and AA in that it utilizes a twelve-step program, but their program is specifically designed around faith. If you or your child is religious, then Celebrate Recovery may be a good choice for you, particularly if your child has found support at church, or if their faith helps them to stay clean or sober. They use Step Studies, The Journey Begins, and The Journey Continues to denote different levels of their program, and the CR program is open to anyone who has struggled with substance or alcohol abuse.

As you can see, there are quite a few options available for you, your family and your kid. Your best bet may be to try several of these options to find the one that works the best and is in line with the way that you want to handle your kid's substance abuse and the way that they see themselves moving forward in recovery. If finances are a problem, the free meetings are a wonderful option for finding support and hope, without having to pay for something that you or your family cannot afford.

Remember that this is a limited list, and there may be more available options for you. Ask your therapist what they would recommend and spend some time searching the Internet for options in your area. You may want to begin doing this research immediately upon realizing that your kid has a problem; whether you use Plan A, Plan B, or both, ideally, you do not want there to be a gap in your kid's recovery. Having meetings or programs picked out and ready to attend will help your child stay clean and stay sober from the first day forward.

Key takeaways:

- An ongoing commitment to follow-through is critical for your journey.
- Finding the best option may be a matter of trying several options to find the one that works the best and is in line with the way that you want to handle your kid's substance abuse and healing the family.
- Just because your kid is sober now does not mean the problem is solved. Everyone needs to take care of themselves in order to present in the family.
- There are a ton of options for individual and family recovery; try them out and see which one works for you.
- The best way you can support your kid's recovery is to get serious about your own recovery and mental health. Remember, you cannot expect your kid to do something you are not willing to do.

Appendix 1

12-Step-based Recovery Programs:

Alcoholics Anonymous www.aa.org

Cocaine Anonymous https://www.ca.org

Drug Addicts Anonymous https://www.daausa.org

Al-Anon Family Groups www.al-anon.org

Adult Children of Alcoholics https://adultchildren.org

Codependents Anonymous http://coda.org

Families Anonymous https://www.familiesanonymous.org

Appendix #2

Governing Bodies and Associations for Treatment Programs and Professionals

National Association of Addiction Treatment Providers https://www.naatp.org

The Independent Educational Consultants Association (IECA) https://www.iecaonline.com

National Association of Therapeutic Schools and Programs https://natsap.org

Association of Intervention Specialists

https://www.associationofinterventionspecialists.org

NAADAC, Association for Addiction Professionals

https://www.naadac.org

Appendix # 3

Dr. Kevin McCauley's 10 Principles:

1 – **90 Days of Residential Treatment.** It has been demonstrated that 30 and 60 days of treatment are insufficient to provide a solid foundation for recovery. A full 90 days in a residential program provides a strong base for ongoing recovery.

2 – **Seamless Transition into a Sober Living Environment.** McCauley emphasizes that the addict should visit sober living houses — and choose the one he or she will move into — while still in residential treatment. Upon release from the inpatient facility, the recovering addict should be transported directly to the sober living environment so there is no time during this vulnerable transition for the addict to obtain drugs or alcohol.

3 – **Frequent, Non-Random Drug Testing.** Drug testing must continue throughout the first year of recovery and be performed at frequent enough intervals to detect any time the addict uses his or her drug of choice. Any lower frequency gives the addict a window in which to use with impunity, which is a disservice to the recovering addict: a clean test enhances motivation for recovery.

4 – **Outpatient Treatment Program.** While the addict is residing in a sober living environment after being released from residential care, he or she needs to continue treatment. This will entail working with a drug addiction counselor and may include individual, family and/or group therapy.

5 – **A Relapse Prevention Plan**. A recovering addict may be exposed to old triggers to drink or use, and new situations are likely to arise in which he or she will have impulses to use again. Very early in outpatient treatment — if this has not been done during the residential stay — it is helpful for an addict, in the presence of his or her therapist, to draw up a relapse prevention plan that spells out in detail who to call, where to go and what to do when impulses to use arise. The addict should write out his or her plan, carry it at all times, and use it religiously as needed.

6 – **90 AA Meetings in 90 Days**. "90 in 90" means that the addict should attend at least 90 meetings in his first 90 days of being in outpatient treatment. This gives the recovering addict a firm footing in the recovery community of Alcoholics Anonymous. In the environment of AA, the recovering addict can learn sober ways of thinking, behaving and coping, and observe sober people who are creating sober lives for themselves. AA

offers the addict a community in which to develop personal connections and to feel a sense of belonging.

7 – **Meeting with an Addiction Physician**. There can be medical complications resulting from addiction, and a physician versed in the physical effects of addiction, and the physical changes that accompany recovery, will be best able to help the addict understand and manage his symptoms.

8 – **Meeting with an Addiction Psychiatrist**. There may be psychiatric issues that preceded addiction or that arose during the period of use, and a psychiatrist who is knowledgeable about the psychological issues that accompany drug and alcohol dependence can distinguish psychological symptoms that are transitory aspects of recovery from those that may benefit from psychotropic medication. Sometimes an addict needs a period of time to be sober before a psychiatrist can determine what symptoms are likely to clear up with sobriety.

9 – **Return to Work**. Returning to work is an important aspect of becoming a fully functional after a lapse into addiction. Furthermore, work helps build self-esteem and offset the shame that generally accompanies addiction and job loss. Someone in early recovery may benefit from choosing a lower-stress job than he or she had previously since the goal of working at this phase of recovery is to provide consistency, structure, responsibility and an opportunity to perform well rather than to embark on, or resume, a particular career path. For some people in recovery, return to a previous job is appropriate, but for others, this is not the case. Determining what constitutes appropriate work for a specific individual is

a topic that the recovering addict can person discuss with a therapist or group leader.

10 – **Fun**. The dopamine that has been depleted in addiction needs replenishment. Learning non-drug-using ways to produce pleasure is essential to rebuilding the natural supplies of dopamine. Without dopamine, recovery will not be appealing; the addict will experience more pain than pleasure, and the option of returning to alcohol or drugs in order to feel good will be compelling.

Following these ten principles can be a tall order, which is why the person in recovery, and his or her family, can benefit from substantial support and guidance. A counselor can reinforce these principles and can steer the recovering person to their close adherence, for the sake of building a solid recovery platform.

Made in the USA
Columbia, SC
05 October 2021

46436680R00067